Fat Masons Need Love

A Shocking Masonic Book for Dummies, Idiots and other Generally Stupid Types

A Collection of Side Spliting Masonic Humor

Fat Masons Need Love
Edited by Michael R. Poll

A Cornerstone Book
Published by Cornerstone Book Publishers
Copyright © 1995 & 2007 byMichael R. Poll

Cornerstone Book Publishers
New Orleans, LA

First Cornerstone Edition - 2008

www.cornerstonepublishers.com

ISBN: 1-934935-11-5
ISBN 13: 978-1-934935-11-8

MADE IN THE USA

I never drink water because of the disgusting things
that fish do in it.

-- W.C. Fields

Fat Masons
Need Love

Brain Transplant

A young Mason had been suffering from severe headaches and had tests run by his doctor, another Lodge Brother. The doctor said, "I'm sorry Brother, but you have a massive brain tumor."

The young man started crying and said, "I haven't even been through the chairs yet. I don't want to die."

The doctor said, "Well this is modern medicine. There is an experimental technique for a brain transplant, but it's expensive and not covered by insurance."

The young Mason said, "I don't care. How much does it cost?"

The doctor replied, "Well, a Grand Lodge Officer brain is $1,000,000 and a Lodge Officer brain is $25,000."

The young Mason said, "No problem. But why is the Grand Lodge Officer brain so much more expensive then the Lodge Officer brain?" The doctor replied, "Because the Lodge Officer brain is USED!"

Star Meeting

Who are the butcher, the baker, and the candlestick maker?

The only people not introduced at an Eastern Star meeting.

Past Masters

How many Past Masters does it take to screw in a lightbulb?

One, but don't expect results.

Memory Test

Three elderly Past Masters are at the doctor's office for a memory test.

The doctor asks the first man, "What is three times three?" "274," is his reply.

The doctor rolls his eyes and looks up at the ceiling, and says to the second man,

"It's your turn. What is three times three?"

"Tuesday," replies the second man.

The doctor shakes his head sadly, then asks the third man,

"Okay, your turn. What's three times three?"

"Nine," says the third man.

"That's great!" says the doctor. "How did you get that?"

"Simple," he says, "just subtract 274 from Tuesday."

Shrine Heaven

Why do only 10% of all Shriners go to heaven?

Because if they all went it would be hell!

Late, Late, Late

WB. Tom, one of the lodge's most respected PMs, was in his early 50s, retired and started a second career.

However, he just couldn't seem to get to work on time. Every day, 5, 10, 15 minutes late. But he was a good worker, real sharp, so the Boss was in a quandary about how to deal with it. Finally, one day he called him into the office for a talk.

"Tom, I have to tell you, I like your work ethic, you do a bang-up job, but you're being late so often is quite bothersome."

"Yes, I know, Boss, and I am working on it."

"Well good, you are a team player. That's what I like to hear. It's odd though, you coming in late. I know you're retired from the Marines. What did they say if you came in late there?"

They said, "Good morning, General."

Wrong Way!

Returning to his hotel room after a too many drinks, the drunk Shriner walked into the elevator shaft and promptly dropped five stories. Lying bloodied and broken and flat on his back, he stared back along the shaft and sneered, "I wanted to go up, dammit!"

What's in a Name?

The new WM was invited to the lodge's Senior PM's home for dinner.

The old PM preceded every request to his wife by endearing terms, calling her Honey, My Love, Darling, Sweetheart, Pumpkin, etc.

The WM was impressed since he knew the couple had been married almost 70 years, and while the wife was off in the kitchen he said to the PM, "I think it's wonderful that after all the years you've been married, you still call your wife those pet names."

The old PM hung his head. "To tell you the truth, I forgot her name about ten years ago."

The Lecture

There's a man, walking down the street at one in the morning and he's very drunk. A policeman stops him and asks: Where are you going in that condition?

Man: II'mm on mmyy waayyy to a lectttuurre on FFreemmassonnrrry.

Officer: Where can you possibly get a lecture on Freemasonry at this time of night?

Man: Frromm mmyy wifffe, wwhenn I gget homme!

Picky Eaters

One cannibal said to the other, "You know, I really can't stand Masons."

"To hell with them, then," said the other. "Just eat the noodles."

10 Things a Shriner Should NEVER Say to a Police Officer

1. I can't reach my license unless you hold my beer. (OK in Texas)
2. Sorry, Officer, I didn't realize my radar detector wasn't plugged in.
3. Aren't you the guy from the Village People?
4. Hey, you must've been doin' about 125 mph to keep up with me. Good job!
5. Are You Andy or Barney?
6. I thought you had to be in relatively good physical condition to be a police officer.
7. You're not gonna check the trunk, are you?
8. Gee, Officer! That's terrific. The last officer only gave me a warning, too!
9. I was trying to keep up with traffic. Yes, I know there are no other cars around. That's how far ahead of me they are.
10. When the Officer says "Gee Sir....Your eyes look red, have you been drinking?" You probably shouldn't respond with,"Gee Officer your eyes look glazed, have you been eating doughnuts?"

Chili Cook Off

Recently Frank, a Shriner from New Hampshire, was vacationing in Texas and was honored to be selected as a judge at a chili cooking contest. The original person called in sick at the last moment and Bro. Frank happened to be standing there at the judge's table asking for directions to the Coors Light truck, when the call came in. He was assured by the other two judges (native Texans) that the chili wouldn't be all that spicy and, besides, they told him that he could have free beer during the tasting, so he accepted. Here are the scorecards from the event:

Chili #1 Eddie's Maniac Monster Chili...

Judge #1 -- A little too heavy on the tomato. Amusing kick.

Judge #2 -- Nice, smooth tomato flavor. Very mild.

Judge #3 -- (Frank) What the hell is this stuff?! It could remove dried paint from your driveway. Took me two beers to put out the flames. I hope that's the worst one. These Texans are crazy!

Chili #2 Austin's Afterburner Chili...

Judge #1 -- Smoky, with a hint of pork. Slight jalapeno tang.

Judge #2 -- Exciting BBQ flavor; needs more peppers to be taken seriously.

Judge #3 -- Keep this out of the reach of children. I'm not sure what I'm supposed to taste besides pain. I had to wave off two people who wanted to give me the Heimlich maneuver. They had to rush in more beer when they saw the look on my face.

Chili #3 Ronny's Famous Burn Down the Barn Chili...

Judge #1 -- Excellent firehouse chili. Great kick. Needs mo\
beans.

Judge #2 -- A beanless chili, a bit salty, good use of peppers.

Judge #3 -- Call the EPA. I've located a uranium spill. My nose feels like I have been snorting Drano. Everyone knows the routine by now. Get me more beer before I ignite. Barmaid pounded me on the back, now my backbone is in the front part of my chest. I'm getting pie-eyed from all of the beer...

Chili #4 Dave's Black Magic...

Judge #1 -- Black bean chili with almost no spice. Disappointing.

Judge #2 -- Hint of lime in the black beans. Good side dish for fish, or other mild foods; not much of a chili.

Judge #3 -- I felt something scraping across my tongue, but was unable to taste it. Is it possible to burn out taste buds? Sally, the barmaid, was standing behind me with fresh refills. That 300 pound woman is starting to look hot ... just like this nuclear waste I'm eating! Is chili an aphrodisiac?

Chili #5 Lisa's Legal Lip Remover...

Judge #1 -- Meaty, strong chili. Cayenne peppers freshly ground, adding considerable kick. Very impressive.

Judge #2 -- Chili using shredded beef, could use more to-

...ato. Must admit the cayenne peppers make a strong statement.

Judge #3 -- My ears are ringing, sweat is pouring off my forehead, and I can no longer focus my eyes. I farted and four people behind me needed paramedics. The contestant seemed offended when I told her that her chili had given me brain damage. Sally saved my tongue from bleeding by pouring beer directly on it from the pitcher. I wonder if I'm burning my lips off. It really pisses me off that the other judges asked me to stop screaming. Screw those rednecks.

Chili #6 Pam's Very Vegetarian Variety...

Judge #1 -- Thin, yet bold vegetarian variety chili. Good balance of spices and peppers.

Judge #2 -- The best yet. Aggressive use of peppers, onions, and garlic. Superb.

Judge #3 -- My intestines are now a straight pipe filled with gaseous, sulfuric flames. I pooped on myself when I farted and I'm worried it will eat through the chair! No one seems inclined to stand behind me anymore. I need to wipe my butt with a snow cone.

Chili #7 Carla's Screaming Sensation Chili...

Judge #1 -- A mediocre chili with too much reliance on canned peppers.

Judge #2 -- Ho-hum; tastes as if the chef literally threw in a can of chili peppers at the last moment. **I should take note that I am worried about Judge #3. He appears to be in a bit of distress as he is cursing uncontrollably.

Judge #3 -- You could put a grenade in my mouth, pull the pin, and I wouldn't feel a thing. I've lost sight in one eye, and the world sounds like it is made of rushing water. My shirt is covered with chili, which slid unnoticed out of my mouth. My pants are full of lava to match my shirt. At least during the autopsy, they'll know what killed me. I've decided to stop breathing; it's too painful. Screw it; I'm not getting any oxygen anyway. If I need air, I'll just suck it in through the four-inch hole in my stomach.

Chili #8 Karen's Toenail Curling Chili...

Judge #1 -- The perfect ending, this is a nice blend chili. Not too bold, but spicy enough to declare its existence.

Judge #2 -- This final entry is a good, balanced chili. Neither mild, nor hot. Sorry to see that most of it was lost when Judge #3 farted, passed out, fell over, and pulled the chili pot down on top of himself. Not sure if he's going to make it. Poor fella, wonder how he'd have reacted to really hot chili?

Judge #3 -- Oh, God ...

Popcorn

How many Masons does it take to pop popcorn?

Three. One to hold the pan and two others to show off and shake the stove.

Grand Lodge Above

Pat & Bill had been Lodge Brothers for many years. They had promised each other long ago that the first to go to the Grand Lodge above would return to tell the other whether there really were Lodges in Heaven and what they were like. By and by, it came to pass that Bill went first.

One day shortly after, Pat was working in his garden when he heard a whispered voice, "Pssst Pat!" He looked around but saw nothing. A few moments later he heard, now quite clearly

"Pat! It's me, Bill!"

"Bill" Pat exclaimed, "are you in Heaven?"

"Indeed I am " said Bill.

Pat paused for a while to get over the shock and then said, "Well, Bill, are there Lodges up there in Heaven?"

"There certainly are, Pat. There are Lodges all over and they are quite magnificent, equal or better to Great Queen Street. The meetings are well attended, the ritual is letter perfect, the festive board fantastic and the spirit of Masonic Fellowship is all pervasive."

"My goodness, Bill," said Pat, "It certainly sounds very impressive but for all that you seem rather sad. Tell me old friend, what is the matter."

"Well, Pat, you are right. I have some good news and some bad."

"OK, Whats the good news?"

"The good news is that we are doing a 3rd this coming Wednesday"

"Great" said Pat. "What's the bad news then?"

"You're the Senior Deacon!"

Found on a Cup in a Lodge in Ireland

"OLD MASONS NEVER DIE, BUT YOU'LL HAVE TO JOIN TO FIND OUT WHY

The Fishing Trip

Two Lodge Members are out fishing and they are having great luck. They are catching so fast that they they have to go back early.

"This is so great," says the first guy. "We should mark the spot so we can come here again."

"You're right," says the other guy who then dives over the side and paints a big X on the bottom of the boat.

They head back to shore and just as they're about to dock, the first guy looks at the second guy and says,

"But what if we don't get the same boat next time?"

The Sober One

Some few years back, just after the introduction of Random Breath Testing, the Police officers of a small country township had to show the community that the RBT was working. They decided to stake out the local Masonic Hall, then as the night wore on, eventually a mason slowly came down the stairs and got into his car.

The moment he started the engine the two officers approached him and asked him to "blow into the bag". He did of course but to the amazement of the officers proved negative.

Fearing a faulty bag, they tried again with the same results. Sure of a possible conviction they then escorted him to the Police station to do a blood test, with it also proving negative.

Being upset with this they then asked him what had gone on and what he had done that evening, to which he answered, "The Grand Master was there, the Grand Secretary was there, the Grand Stewards were there and we all had a great time.

Puzzled, the officers asked him if he had a Grand Lodge position.

"My position?" he answered "I'm the Grand Decoy."

Heavenly Wings

A Mason and a Shriner died and both went to heaven where they were issued their wings with the warning that if they had even have one bad thought their wings would fall off.

Well, everything went well for some time then one day they passed a very attractive and well put together young lady.

As the Mason turned to watch her pass his wings fell off.

When the Mason bent over to pick them up the Shriner's wings fell off.

Practice, Practice, Practice

While Brother Joe was visiting a newly initiated brother at home one evening, his wife took him to one side and said her husband had started behaving very strange since joining. He asked in what way?

She said, "He locks himself in the bathroom for hours on end mumbling to himself with his little blue book."

As the evening proceeded I asked him about the lodge, and him how he was getting on.

"Oh fine" he answered. I asked him about his bathroom conversations and asked if there any thing wrong.

"No", he said. So why read the book there?

"Well," he said "Its the only TYLED room in the house."

Parrot Ritual

A Mason was having trouble with his ritual, and was telling a fellow mason in a bar one day. His friend said that he knows a guy down the road who sells Parrots who know the ritual and promp you when you have any trouble.

So the next day off he went to the shop. The man pulled a curtain open and there were 3 parrots, one with a MM's apron on, one with a WM's apron, and one with a grand lodge apron on.

He said "How much is the one with the WM's apron on?"

"$2000 and he knows all the ritual including the inner workings, and will always promp you when you get stuck.

"No", he said "too expensive", "what about the one with the MM apron on?"

"Well, that one is $1,000 and he knows all the ritual, but not the inner workings, but will always promp you when you are learning it."

"No, too much. What about the one with the grand lodge apron on?"

"You can have him for $10.00."

"Why so cheap? He must know all the ritual and the inner workings?"

"Oh yes, he knows all the ritual, but when you make a mistake all he does is sit there and shake his head!!

Grand Officers

Why do some people take an instant aversion to Grand Officers?

It saves time in the long run.

Important Things in Life

An ambitious yuppie Mason finally decided to take a vacation. He booked himself on a Caribbean cruise and proceeded to have the time of his life—at least for a while.

A hurricane came unexpectedly. The ship went down and was lost instantly. The man found himself swept up on the shore of an island with no other people, no supplies, nothing. Only bananas and coconuts.

Used to four-star hotels, this guy had no idea what to do. So for the next four months he ate bananas, drank coconut juice, longed for his old life and fixed his gaze on the sea, hoping to spot a rescue ship.

One day, as he was lying on the beach, he spotted movement out of the corner of his eye. It was a rowboat, and in it was the most gorgeous woman he had ever seen.

She rowed up to him. In disbelief, he asked her: "Where did you come from? How did you get here?"

"I rowed from the other side of the island," she said. "I landed here when my cruise ship sank."

"Amazing," he said, "I didn't know anyone else had survived. How many of you are there? You were really lucky to have a rowboat wash up with you."

"It's only me," she said, "and the rowboat didn't wash up nothing did."

He was confused, "Then how did you get the rowboat?"

"Oh, simple," replied the woman. "I made it out of raw material that I found on the island. The oars were whittled from gum-tree branches, I wove the bottom from palm branches, and the sides and stern came from a eucalyptus tree."

"But, but, that's impossible," stuttered the man. "You had no tools or hardware—how did you manage?"

"Oh, that was no problem," the woman said. "On the south side of the island, there is a very unusual stratum of exposed alluvial rock. I found that if I fired it to a certain temperature in my kiln, it melted into forgeable ductile iron. I used that for tools, and used the tools to make the hardware. But enough of that. Where do you live?" Sheepishly, the man confessed that he had been sleeping on the beach the whole time.

"Well, let's row over to my place, then," she said.

After a few minutes of rowing, she docked the boat at a small wharf. As the man looked onto shore, he nearly fell out of the boat. Before him was a stone walk leading to an exquisite bungalow painted in blue and white.

While the woman tied up the rowboat with an expertly woven hemp rope, the man could only stare ahead, dumbstruck. As they walked into the house, she said casually, "It's not much, but I call it home. Sit down, please would you like to have a drink?"

"No, no, thank you," he said, still dazed. "I can't take any more coconut juice."

"It's not coconut juice," the woman replied. "I have a still. How about a pina colada?"

Trying to hide his continued amazement, the man accepted, and they sat down on her couch to talk.

After they had exchanged their stories, the woman announced, "I'm going to slip into something more comfortable. Would you like to take a shower and shave? There is a razor upstairs in the cabinet in the bathroom."

No longer questioning anything, the man went into the bathroom. There in the cabinet was a razor made from a bone handle. Two shells honed to a hollow-ground edge were fastened to its tip, inside a swivel mechanism. "This woman is amazing," he mused. "What next?"

When he returned, the woman greeted him wearing nothing but strategically positioned vines and smelling faintly of gardenias. She beckoned for him to sit down next to her.

"Tell me," she began suggestively, slithering closer to him, "We've been out here for a very long time. You've been lonely. There's something I'm sure you really feel like doing right now, something you've been longing for all these months? You know."

She stared into his eyes. He couldn't believe what he was hearing.

"You mean..." he replied, "I can really check my e-mail and the Freemason-List from here?"

We Could Have Been Here Sooner

An elderly Past Master and his wife were killed in an accident and found themselves being given a tour of heaven by Saint Peter. "Here is your oceanside condo, over there are the tennis courts, swimming pool, and two golf courses. If you need any refreshments, just stop by any of the many bars located throughout the area."
"Heck, Gloria," the old man hissed when Saint Peter walked off, "we could have been here ten years ago if you hadn't heard about all that stupid oat bran, wheat germ, and low-fat diets!"

Posted Above the WM's Station

Some drink at the fountain of knowledge. Others just gargle.

Price of a Peek

It seems a Jewish family rented an apartment that sat directly under the Masonic Temple, and at least once a month they would always hear this stomping from above. One day Izzy told his wife he was going to drill a hole in the ceiling and see what those Masons were up to. After doing so, one evening he heard some stomping coming from above, so he got his ladder, climbed up and decided to take a peek. After a few moments, he flew down the ladder and ran in and told his wife to pack all their belongs and "Let's get out of here and fast!!!" When she asked why, Izzy told her that he was just peeking in on the Masons above and saw them kill a man and said they were going to blame it on the 'JEW-BELOW'.

Light Blubs, Light Bulbs

Q: How many Masons does it take to unscrew a light bulb?
A: It's a secret!

Q: How many Masons does it take to screw in a light bulb?
A: Three. One to screw it in, one to read the minutes of the previous light bulb replacement, and one to sit on the sidelines and complain that this wasn't the way they used to screw in light bulbs.

Q. How many Masons does it take to change a light bulb?
A. After much research this tricky question can now be answered. It takes 20, as follows:

2 to complain that the light doesn't work.
1 to pass the problem to either another committee, the Temple Board or the Master of the Lodge.
3 to do a study on light in the Lodge.
2 to check out the types of lights the Knights of Columbus use.
3 to argue about it.
5 to plan a fund-raising dinner to raise money for the bulb.
2 to complain that the new bulb is not like the ones in the past.
1 to borrow a ladder, donate the bulb and install it.
1 to order the brass memorial plate and have it inscribed.

Q: How many Past Masters does it take to change a light bulb?
A: Change it! Why?

Sound Light

Light travels faster than sound.

This is why some Masons appear bright until you hear them speak.

Those Western Masons

In the days of the old west, a young fellow held up a bank, and in so doing shot and killed the teller. Several people in the bank and outside saw him well enough to identify him as he rode out of town. A possee was formed and in short order had captured him and brought him to jail. He was duly tried and sentenced to hang for his crime.

On the appointed day a scaffold had been erected outside the jail. The fellow was lead up the steps to the scaffold, the Judge read his sentence, and asked the fellow if he had anything to say.

"I sure do, Judge. If it wasn't for the dang Masons I wouldn't be here."

The Judge inquired to what he referred.

"Well, the Sheriff who pursued me is a Mason, as were most of the possee. The jury was mostly Masons, and you, Judge, are a Mason. If it wasn't for the dang Masons I wouldn't be here."

That being all he had to say, the Judge ordered the hangman to proceed. The hangman put a HOOD over his head, a ROPE around his neck, took him by the right arm and said, "Take one regular step forward with your left foot."

God's Mail

A postman, on his route, picked up a letter from a mailbox that was addressed to God. The postman seeing that the letter was not sealed, and there being no postage on it, opened and read it.

It was from a man who was down on his luck and was asking God for help. The letter asked for $50 to get his family through the next week.

The postman, being a Mason, took the letter to Lodge that evening, read it, and asked for donations for the unfortunate fellow.

The Masons, wanting to help, took up a collection, and received twenty five dollars from the brethren. The Secretary placed the cash in a Lodge envelope, and gave it to the postman to deliver the following day, which he did.

Another day passed, and the postman again found an unsealed letter in the mailbox addressed to God. Again he opened and read the letter, which thanked God for the money, but instructed him to send it through the Knights of Columbus next time as the Masons kept half.

Last Year's WM

When I die, I want to go like last year's WM did -- in his sleep.

Not screaming like the passengers in his car.

Call Me Tomorrow

A Doctor and Plumber are in the same Lodge. On Sunday Morning the Doctor wakes up to find his toilet blocked. So he rings the Plumber.

"But I don't work Sundays! Can't it wait until tomorrow?"

The Doctor said. "I don't like working Sundays either but if you were in trouble, and felt unwell, Brother I would come round to see you."

"OK" says the Plumber and goes to the Doctor's home. He goes upstairs and looks at the toilet, takes two aspirins from his pocket and throws them down the bowl.

"There, Brother." he says "If it's no better tomorrow give me a ring and I will come back."

The Knocking Tiler

Have you heard of the Lodge that was holding its meetings in the ball room of the local hotel while its building was under-going renovations? One night a traveling salesman asked the desk clerk who all those men going into the room were.

The desk clerk replied "Oh, those are the Masons."

The salesman said, "Oh, I've always wanted to join that lodge. Do you think they would let me in?" "

Oh, I don't know," said the clerk. "They're awful exclusive. Why, you see that poor guy standing outside the door with a sword? He's been knocking for four hours and they still won't let him in!!!"

The Game

A man is walking through the recreation ground of his local park when he notices a huge game in full fury on the football field he is passing.

"What's going on?" he asks a spectator watching from the side-lines.

The other replies "It's a match between the Masons and the Knights of Columbus."

"What's the score?" asks the first man.

"I don't know, it's a secret."

Ready for the 2nd

A little before Lodge is about to open an old man totters up to the Tyler and says, " I'm here to receive my 2nd degree."

Well, they all look at this guy, who is really older than dirt, and they ask him to explain.

"I was given my EA degree on July 4, 1922. Now I'm ready for my 2nd degree."

So they go scurrying for the records, and sure enough, there was his name, entered on July 4, 1922.

"Where have you been all these years? What took you so long to be ready for your 2nd?" they ask.

He replied: "I was learning to subdue my passions!"

A Cold One

A small Lodge had had a string of bad luck. It was preparing to initiate a candidate on a steamy evening in August and it's air conditioner stopped working.

After sweating their way through part of the work, the Master had asked the candidate what he most desired.

The candidate replied "a beer".

At this juncture the Senior Deacon, being startled, whispered "light" to the candidate.

"OK," the candidate replied, "a lite beer."

The "Caught" Degree

Bro. John and Bro. Joe are getting ready for a lodge meeting. When John takes his apron out of the case, Joe notices a pair of silk stockings hanging out of the case.

Joe asks: "Hey John, what's this with the ladies stuff?"

John gives a quick look and whispers: "You remember the installation meeting last year?"

Joe acknowledges and John goes on:

"Keep it a secret, but on the way home I stopped at the pub where I met this lovely woman. Apparently she lost her stockings in my car, and my wife found them. I told my wife I was passed to a higher degree, and ever since she takes them out of the case washes them and puts them back in with my gloves!"

The Hands of "Time"

It seems that another Mason, WM of his Lodge, went to Heaven and met with St. Peter. He identified himself as a member of the Craft and St. Peter asked, "What Lodge?"

Proudly the Master replied, "Old Adage Lodge No. 1."

St. Peter immediately took him to the Masonic Clock Room.

The Master, in puzzlement, looked around the room which was filled with clocks. Each clock had a Lodge's name on a brass plate and, strangely enough, each clock was at a different time.

He asked why and St. Peter informed him that the hands only moved when someone in that Lodge made a mistake in the Ritual.
The Master then asked where his Lodge's clock was as he couldn't see it.

St. Peter replied, "Why, it's in the kitchen, of course."

"The kitchen," said the Master?

"Yes, you see, we needed a new fan."

Love

EA: "My wife is an angel."

PM: "Lucky you. Mine's still alive."

4 Masons In A Car

There are 4 Masons in a car, 1 from Iowa,1 from Wisconsin, 1 from Florida, and 1 from Illinois.

The Mason from Florida says "I'm tired of seeing oranges everyday" so he throws some oranges out the window.

So then the Mason from Iowa says "I'm tired of seeing Corn everyday" so he throws some corn out the window.

The Mason from Wisconsin is very inspired so he opens the door and pushs the Brother from Illinois out of the car!

Nice Words

A Mason walks into a bar, sits down, and orders a drink.

"Hey, nice tie!" comes out of nowhere.

He looks up at the bartender to see if he had said anything, but since he was on the other side of the bar the Mason just ignores it.

"Hey! Nice shirt!"

The Mason looks up but, again, the bartender is engaged elsewhere.

"Hey! Nice suit!"

The Mason then calls the bartender over and asks him if he keeps talking to him.

"It's not me, it's the complimentary peanuts."

The English Language

In old New Orleans, the Masons in the 1800's could not agree if they should work in the French or English language.

A French Mason complained that the English language makes no sense at all and gave a list of examples to support his claim.

1- The bandage was wound around the wound.
2- The farm was used to produce produce.
3- The dump was so full that it had to refuse more refuse.
4- We must polish the Polish furniture.
5- He could lead if he would get the lead out.
6- The soldier decided to desert his dessert in the desert.
7- Since there is no time like the present, he thought it was time to
present the present.
8- A bass was painted on the head of the bass drum.
9- When shot at, the dove dove into the bushes.
10- I did not object to the object.
11- The insurance was invalid for the invalid.
12- There was a row among the oarsmen about how to row.
13- They were too close to the door to close it.
14- The buck does funny things when the does are present.
15- A seamstress and a sewer fell down into a sewer line.
16- To help with planting, the farmer taught his sow to sow.
17- The wind was too strong to wind the sail
18- After a number of injections my jaw got number.
19- Upon seeing the tear in the painting I shed a tear.
20- I had to subject the subject to a series of tests.
21- How can I intimate this to my most intimate friend?
22- I want it to be on record that I will record my record

Prompt Him!

A Mason is on a Business Trip. One day he comes to a small village, somewhere in the north of England. Our Brother is curious to know whether there is a Masonic Lodge or not, so he takes a walk through the village and after some time he finds a path called "Mason's Road". Thinking that the path might lead to the Masonic Temple, he follows it. At the end of the pathway he sees a building, which looks somewhat rotten and seems to have been out of use for quite a while.

Our Brother tries to open the door and, surprisingly, it is not locked. He goes inside and finds dust and spider webs everywhere. In front a door there sits a skeleton, wearing an apron, a collar and holding a sword in its hand. "O my God", thinks our Brother and enters the Lodge room.

In puzzlement, he sees skeletons with collars and aprons everywhere. The W.M., the Wardens, the Organist, Deacons - all skeletons. He looks around and goes to the seats of the Secretary and Treasurer.

Under the hand of the Treasurer he finds a small piece of paper, a little note, which he seems to have passed to the Secretary. So our Brother picks up the note, blows away the dust and reads: "If nobody prompts the W.M., we will sit here forever!"

The *Real* Boss

A wife heard her husband come back into the house not too long after he had left for the night. She said, "Honey, I thought you were going to your lodge meeting."

"It was postponed." He replied. "The wife of the Most Worshipful Grand Master wouldn't let him attend tonight."

Wise Genie

The Worshipful Master of a Lodge found a bottle with a Genie in it. In accordance with custom, the Genie offered to grant him a wish.

"OK," said the WM, "I've always wanted to go to Hawaii, but I hate to fly. So my wish is for you to build a bridge so I can drive to Hawaii."

"I can't do that!!!" exclaimed the Genie. "Don't you know that's impossible? No Genie could do that. It's too far, the water is too deep, it's just totally beyond anybody's power. You will have to make another wish."

"OK," said the Master. "I wish that at our next Stated Meeting all the old PMs would just get along and not cause any trouble, not have to tell us how they did it their year, not complain about the ritual, not put down the current officers ... just sit on the sidelines and behave!"

"Hmmmmm," said the Genie. "Do you want that bridge with 2 lanes or 4??"

The Masonic Ticket

Police officer, writing a speeding ticket: "I see by your car emblem that you are a Fast Master..."

Billing

Two Lodge Brothers, a doctor and a lawyer, were talking at a party. Their conversation was constantly interrupted by people describing their ailments and asking the doctor for free medical advice. After an hour of this, the exasperated doctor asked the lawyer, "What do you do to stop people from asking you for legal advice when you're out of the office?"

"I give it to them," replied the lawyer, "and then I send them a bill." The doctor was shocked, but agreed to give it a try. The next day, still feeling slightly guilty, the doctor prepared the bills. When he went to place them in his mailbox, he found a bill from the lawyer.

The EA

After receiving his enterred apprentice degree the candidate returned home. His wife asked him what happened to him.

Recalling that he couldn't give up the secrets of that degree all he could muster was, "Well honey, there were a lot of walkers, talkers and preachers."

With a somewhat confused look on her face she asked what he meant.

He explained, "Well, I couldn't see anybody in the room and was guided around. I would stop then somebody would talk. Then I was guided around by someone else, was stopped, then somebody else talked."

His wife then asked, "That explains the walkers and talkers ... what about the preachers?"

He pondered for a moment then finally replied, "Well, often when somebody finished talking I would hear some other people whispering 'Awwwwww, *God!*'

Bad Drivers

A older Brother is driving on the highway when his wife calls him on his cell phone. "Honey, be carful. I heard on the news that there is a car on the road driving the wrong way." To this the PM replies, "One? Theres millions of 'em!"

Guaranteed Delivery

An older PM took a package to the post office to mail and was told it would cost $6.95 for fast delivery or $4.30 for slower service.

"There is no hurry," he told the clerk, "just so the package is delivered in my lifetime."

He glanced at him and said, "That will be $6.95, please."

Blond

A elderly Past Master walks into a bar and while being served, asks whether anyone would mind him telling a "blond" joke.

The woman behind the bar replied "Well, you can tell a blond joke in here but bear in mind I am blond, my partner over there is blond, the woman sitting next to you is the County mud wrestling champion and is blond, the woman sitting the other side of you is a karate instructor and she's blond and the woman whose just walked in has just been let out for murder and she's blond too. So do you think you really want to tell a blond joke?"

"No" said the old PM. "Not if I am going to have to repeat the punch line five times"

Experienced Dog

Have you heard the story about that fellow who wants to go hunting? He needed a dog and consulted a Brother. That brother, who sold dogs, gave him one, called JW. "It's a very good dog", he said, "he knows a lot about hunting and you can truly rely on him".

Our fellow took the dog. One week later he returned. "It's not too bad, but he doesn't seem to be very experienced. Haven't you got another dog?"

"Sure I have", said the Brother. "This one is called SW and he's a bit more experienced. Try him and if you don't like him, feel free to come back."

Indeed, our fellow returned the dog two weeks later. "He's quite good actually, but he's not what I'm looking for. I need a dog which is more experienced."

"Well", said the Brother, "I can offer you a really experienced dog. He's called PM and you'll have good time with him."

So our fellow took the animal but just one day later he returned. "What's wrong with him?", the Brother asked, "I haven't got any dog that is more experienced than this one."

"Well," our fellow said, "he might be experienced, but all he's doing is sitting there and barking!"

Sigh ...

There is a Mason dressed like a cowboy and a cowboy in the kitchen. Which one is the real cowboy?

The one on the range.

32

The Airplane Ride

A Mason farmer and his wife went to a fair. The farmer was fascinated by the airplanes and asked a pilot how much a ride would cost.

"$10 for 3 minutes," replied the pilot.

"That's too much," said the farmer.

The pilot thought for a second and then said, "I'll make you a deal. If you and your wife ride for 3 minutes without uttering a sound, the ride will be free. But if you make a sound, you'll have to pay $10."

The farmer and his wife agreed and went for a wild ride. After they landed, the pilot said to the farmer, "I want to congratulate you for not making a sound. You are a brave man."

"Maybe so," said the farmer, "But I gotta tell ya, I almost screamed when my wife fell out."

Sad Truth

Brother Philip is telling his friends about his recent divorce.

"Yes, it's true. Sylvie divorced me for religious reasons.

She worshipped money and I didn't have any."

Why Rednecks Don't Make Good Paramedics

A couple of redneck Masons are out in the woods hunting when Bubba suddenly grabs his chest and falls to the ground. He doesn't seem to be breathing; his eyes are rolled back in his head.

Billy Bob whips out his cell phone and calls 911. He gasps to the operator, "I think Bubba is dead! What should I do?"

The operator, in a calm soothing voice says, "Just take it easy and follow my instructions. First, let's make sure he's dead."

There is a silence ... and then a gun shot is heard. The guy's voice comes back on the line, "Okay, now what?"

Posted in the GM Office

Genius does what it must, talent does what it can, and you had best do what you're told.

The Confessional

A drunk Shriner staggered into a Catholic church and sat down in a confession box, saying nothing.

The bewildered priest coughed to attract his attention, but still the Shriner said nothing.

The priest then knocked on the wall three times in a final attempt to get the man to speak.

Finally, the Shriner replied, "No use knocking, there's no paper in this one either."

The Wild Ride

While on holiday in Texas a Past Master decides to try horse-back riding, even though he has had no lessons or prior experience. He mounts the horse, unassisted, and the horse immediately springs into motion.

It gallops along at a steady and rhythmic pace, but the PM begins to slip from the saddle. In terror, he grabs for the horse's mane, but cannot seem to get a firm grip. He tries to throw his arms around the horse's neck, but he slides down the side of the horse anyway.

The horse gallops along, seemingly unaware of its slipping rider. Finally, giving up his frail grip, the PM attempts to leap away from the horse and throw himself to safety. Unfortunately, his foot has become entangled in the stirrup, he is now at the mercy of the horse's pounding hooves as his head is struck against the ground over and over.

As his head is battered against the ground, he is mere moments away from unconsciousness when to his great fortune.... Frank, the Wal-Mart greeter, sees the Past Master's dilemma and unplugs the horse.

The Question

A Mason is driving down the road and his wifes asks:

"Do you ever notice that when you're driving, anyone going slower than you is an idiot and everyone driving faster than you is a maniac?"

Square Boss

A fellow went for an interview for a job. Knowing that the Boss was a prominent Mason he decided to use his position as a newly raised MM to see if it would help him get the job. Off he went with Masonic ring, cufflinks, and S&C tie to the interview. He stood erect and took three steps forward to shake hands with the prospective boss. All though the interview he dropped into the conversation as many references to masonry that he could. At the end the Boss said, "So, if I offer you this position, what do you expect as a package?" The chap thought that his luck was on, and so he said, "A $350,000 per annum and six weeks holiday." To which the boss replied, "We will halve it, and you begin!"

Biting Nails

Two golden-agers were discussing their Past Master husbands over tea.

"I do wish that my Elmer would stop biting his nails. He makes me terribly nervous."

"My Billy used to do the same thing," the older woman replied. "But I broke him of the habit."

"How?"

"I hid his teeth."

Bad Luck

An old Past Master has been slipping in and out of a coma for months, yet his wife stayed by his bedside every single day.

One day, he comes to. He motioned for her to come nearer and with tears welling in his eyes he whispers "You know what? You have been with me through all the bad times. When I got fired. You comforted me. When my business failed, you supported me. When I got shot, you nursed me to health. When we lost the house, you endured living in a shabby doss house. Now my health is failing, you are still right by my side. You know what?"

"What dear?" she asks eagerly.

"I think you're bad luck; why don't you buzz off!"

Hell

A tired old mason whose hair was gray,
Came to the gates of Heaven one day,
When asked, what on earth he had done the most,
He said he had replied to the Visitors Toast.
St. Peter said, as he tolled the Bell,
Come inside my Brother you've had enough of Hell.

Shriner Clowns

Why aren't you allowed to incinerate Shriner Clowns?

They burn funny.

The New Senior Deacon

Pat and Bill had been Lodge Brothers for many years. They had promised each other long ago that the first to go the the Grand Lodge above would return to tell the other whethre there really were Lodges in Heaven and what they were like. By and by, it came to pass the Bill went first.

One day shortly after, Pat was working in his garden when he heard a whispered voice, "Pssst Pat!"

Pat looked around but saw nothing, A few moments later he heard, now quite clearly "Pat its me, Bill!"

"Bill", exclaimed Pat, "are you in Heaven?"

"Indeed I am", said Bill

Pat paused for awhile to get over the shock and then said "Well, Bill, are there Lodges up there in Heaven?"

"There certainly are, Pat. there are Lodge all over and they are quite magnificent, equal or better to Great Queen Street. The meetings are will atended, the ritual is word perfect, the festive board fantastic and the spirit of Masonic Fellowship is all pervasive."

"My goodness, Bill", said Pat, 'It certainly sounds very impressive but for all that you seem rather sad. Tell me old friend what is the matter."

"Well, Pat, you are right. I have some good new and some bad."

"OK, What's the good news?"

"The good news is that we are dong a 2nd Degree this coming Wednesday."

"Great", said Pat. "What's the bad news then?"

"You're the Senior Deacon!"

New Job

A Mason obtained a new job as a salesman and calls his first customer to have a little boy answer the phone.

"Hello, can I please speak to the man of the house?" asks the man

"No" whispers the boy, "he's busy"

"Oh, can I please speak to your mom then?" the salesman asks

"No" replied the little boy, "she's busy"

"Ok, who else can I talk to?"

"The Fire Department" the boy whispers

"Can I speak to the fireman then please?" the salesman asks incredulously

"No" whispers the boy, "he's busy"

"Ok, Ok" the salesman replies, "who else is there I can speak to?"

"The Police" the boy whispers, "But they're busy too"

"What?!" shouts the salesman, "What are they all doing then?"

The little boy replies, still in a whisper "Looking for me"

Went Deaf

An old country Past Master and his wife were out driving one day, when a police officer pulled him over.

"What seems to be the trouble young man?" asked the old gentleman.

As the officer said, "Excuse me sir, but didn't you notice your wife fell out of the car back there?".

To which the old PM exclaimed, "Thank you son, I thought I went deaf!!!".

Too Long

Two lodge Brothers, Bill and Doug, were sitting on a riverbank fishing. They look up at the bridge next to them and see a funeral procession passing over it.

Bill stands up, takes his hat off, holds it over his heart and bows.

Doug said. "That was a very nice thing to do."

"Well" Bill replies. "... we *were* married for 20 years."

For the Road

A Brother was driving home after a Lodge meeting, and a festive board which had consisted of many tastings of wine. Sure enough a blue light followed the car, and he pulled over to the side of the road. Thinking that the policeman might be a Freemason, he placed his driving licenec and insurance documents in his ritual book.

When the police officer asked for his driving licence he made a great play of taking it from his ritual book, but the policeman made no reaction whatsoever. The same with his insurance documents.

He was then asked to blow into the breathalyser which proved positive. He gave the sign of distress, which was ignored. The policeman started to write notes in his pocket book. At this point, the Brother was needing to go to the toilet, so asked the Police Officer if he could retire to the bushes in order to restore himself to his personal comforts. The officer replied, "Certainly sir, and on your return, I shall read to you a charge....."

Where'd They Go?

At the monthly Building Society meeting much discussion raged about the problem of mice in the Lodge building. Of course several sugestions on how to be rid of them were offered. Mouse traps. mouse poison. Buy a cat. Call an exterminator. The building manager took all this advice under consideration and it was agreed that at the next meeting he would make a report on his progress. Sure enough at the next meeting he was questioned. Did you use my idea of a cat? Did you use mine of traps? Finally he said, "All the mice are gone." All wanted to know how he had accomplished such a feat. "Well...I obligated all the mice in as MM and have not seen them since!"

It's All Location

There once was an American who decided to write a book about famous Masonic Lodges around the world.

For his first chapter he decided to write about English lodges. So he booked his tickets and finally arrived in Liverpool, thinking that he would work his way across the country from west to east.

One his first day he was inside a lodge taking photographs when he noticed a golden telephone mounted on the wall with a sign that read, £10,000 per call. The American, being intrigued asked a brother who was strolling by what the telephone was used for. The brother replied that it was a direct line to heaven and that for £10,000 you could talk to the Great Architect. The American thanked the brother and went along his way.

The American's next stop was in Leeds. There while at a very large Masonic Center he saw the same golden telephone with the same sign under it. He wondered if this was the same kind of telephone he saw in Liverpool and he asked a nearby brother what its purpose was. The brother told him that it was a direct line to heaven and that for £10,000 he could talk to the Great Architect. "O.K.,thank you" said the American.

The American traveled on to Leister, Manchester, Birmingham, and many others, and at every Lodge he stopped at he saw the same golden telephone with the same "£10,000 per call" sign under it, and every time the American asked a member of the lodge what the phone was for he got the same answer, "it's a direct line to heaven and for £10,000 you can talk to the Great Architect."

Finally the American arrived at Great Queen Street, and again he saw the same golden telephone but this time the sign under it read "10p. per call." The American was intrigued and he told a Grand Officer, "Most Worshipful Brother, I have traveled all over England and I have seen this same golden telephone in many lodges. I have found out that it is a direct line to heaven, but in all the other cities the cost to call heaven was £10,000. Why is it so cheap here?"

The Most Worshipful Brother smiled and answered, "You are in London now son, it's a local call."

Silent PMs

Q: During a degree, what is the difference between a silent Past Master and a UFO?

A: There have been sightings of UFOs.

Signs

A young Entered Apprentice was being tested on his proficiency. After going over the signs and passwords, he looked at his instructor and asked, "I noticed several of the older members sticking their fingers in their ears and whistling. What does that sign mean?"

"That's not a sign," his instructor said, "Those are Past Masters adjusting their hearing aids."

Hummmm ...

PM: What do you do when a Grand Officer's staggering?

EA: Shoot him again?

Free Drink

A young EA was working part-time as a bartender when a mangy looking guy who goes into the bar and orders a drink.

The bartender says: "No way. I don't think you can pay for it."

The guy says: "You're right. I don't have any money, but if I show you something you haven't seen before, will you give me a drink?"

The EA says, "Only if what you show me ain't risque."

"Deal!" says the guy and reaches into his coat pocket and pulls out a hamster. He puts the hamster on the bar and it runs to the end of the bar, down the bar, across the room, up the piano, jumps on the key board and starts playing Gershwin songs. And the hamster is really good!

The bartender says, "You're right. I've never seen anything like that before. That hamster is truly good on the piano."

The guy downs the drink and asks the bartender for another. "Money or another miracle else no drink", says the bartender.

The guy reaches into his coat again and pulls out a frog. He puts the frog on the bar, and the frog starts to sing. He has a marvelous voice and great pitch. A fine singer!

A stranger from the other end of the bar runs over to the guy and offers him $300 for the frog. The guy says "It's a deal." He takes the three hundred and gives the stranger the frog. The stranger runs out of the bar.

The bartender says to the guy: "Are you some kind of nut? You sold a singing frog for $300? It must have been worth millions. You must be crazy."

"Not so", says the guy. "The hamster is also a ventriloquist."

Numbers

The Eastern Star held a seminar about getting new members. During a break a brother happened to overhear one Worthy Matron say to another, "Ours is up ten." The second Worthy Matron responded, "We've got you beat. Our gain is twenty-five."

The brother said, "Pardon me, sisters. I don't mean to interrupt, but I couldn't help hearing. That's wonderful news! Between your chapters we've got thirty-five new members!"

"New members?" said the first, "We were talking about how many pounds our Worthy Patrons have gained this year."

The Apology

Deep in mid-Wales, two Brothers regularly cycled the 15 miles each way to their Masonic meeting dressed in their dark suits and white shirts. On one occasion one of the bike chains broke and the other stopped to help him get the problem fixed. Both being smartly dressed they couldn't fiddle with the chain, so they searched around in a nearby barn where they found enough cord to fashion a tow rope.

One bike then towed the other the remaining 5 miles to the meeting.

Because of what had happened they arrived late and were admitted into the Lodge room, where they apologized with the following words:-

"Sorry for our lateness Worshipful Master, but we arrived of our own freewheel and a cord"

French Eyes

Recently a UK Lodge had a visitation from a French Lodge and after the Lodge proceedings they all retired to the Festive Board.

The French Director of Ceremonies was seated next to the British DC and conversation about all things ensued. The DC was particularly impressed by the well spoken English of the French Brother and decided that he should at least attempt some conversation in the other's tongue.

Just then a fly alighted on the table and the British DC, pointing to the fly, remarked, "Regarde la Mouche!"

"Ah!", said our continental Brother, "LE Mouche, the fly is male."

At the next Lodge Committee Meeting the DC summing up the visitation said, "Well - I was particularly taken by the French DC's command of English, but what impressed me even more was his fantastic eyesight!"

Carpet

Brother Dave was laying down carpet in an Eastern Star's. As he was finishing, he got a craving for a cigarette. Dave looked around and discovered that his cigarettes were missing. He did, however, notice a bump in the carpet, and figured that he had laid carpet over the pack without noticing it there. Dave decided rather than to take up the carpet, he would get a hammer and pound it into the ground so no one would know.

When he finished that, the owner of the house walked into the room and commented on what a nice job he had done.

"Brother Dave, The carpet looks wonderful!" she exclaimed. "Here are your cigarettes; I found them in the kitchen. Oh yes, and by the way, have you seen my pet gerbil?"

Please God

A drunk Shriner was staggering home with a pint of booze in his back pocket when he slipped and fell heavily. Struggling to his feet, he felt something wet running down his leg.

"Please God", he implored, "let it be blood!"

The Promise

There was a Mason who had worked all of his life and had saved all of his money. He was a real miser when it came to his money. He loved money more than just about anything, and just before he died, he said to his wife, "Now listen, when I die, I want you to take all my money and place it in the casket with me. I wanna take my money to the afterlife."

So he got his wife to promise him with all her heart that when he died, she would put all the money in the casket with him.

Well, one day he died. He was stretched out in the casket, the wife was sitting there in black next to her closest friend. When they finished the ceremony, just before the undertakers got ready to close the casket, the wife said "Wait just a minute!" she had a shoe box with her, she came over with the box and placed it in the casket.

Then the undertakers locked the casket down and rolled it away.

Her friend said, "I hope you weren't crazy enough to put all that money in the casket."

She said, "Yes, I promised. I'm a good christian, I can't lie. I promised him that I was going to put that money in that casket with him."

"You mean to tell me you put every cent of his money in the casket with him?"

"I sure did, " said the wife. "I got it all together, put it into my account and I wrote him a check."

Golfing Brothers

There was an old PM named Bill, and one of the things he most enjoyed was playing golf with his old buddy (another PM) Fred. Bill's wife always commented on how happy he looked after a game.

But one day he came home from their weekly game looking terrible and very tired. His wife asked, "What's the matter, Bill? You always seem so happy after golf and you look miserable right now."

Bill said, "Well, something terrible happened. Fred had a heart attack on the first hole."

"My God, honey!" said the wife, rushing to comfort him. "That must've been terrible!"

"It was," he said. "All day long it was: hit the ball, drag Fred to the ball, and then hit it again..."

The Punishment

A Shriner died and was taken to his place of eternal torment by the devil.

As he passed sulphurous pits and shrieking sinners, he saw a man he recognized as a lawyer and fellow Shriner snuggling up to a beautiful woman.

"That's unfair!" he cried. "I have to roast for all eternity, and that lawyer gets to spend it with a beautiful woman."

"Shut up", barked the devil, jabbing the man with his pitchfork. "Who are you to question that woman's punishment?"

A Real Mason

A Mason went to a bar and ordered a drink. As he sat sipping his whiskey, a young lady sat down next to him. She turned to the Mason, saw his Masonic ring and asked, "Are you a real Mason?"

He replied, "Well, I joined my lodge 15 years ago. I served every office in the line up to Worshipful Master. I've also been a District Deputy Grand Master and serve now as my Lodge Secretary. So yes, I guess I am a real Mason."

She said, "I'm a lesbian. I spend my whole day thinking about women. As soon as I get up in the morning, I think about women; when I shower, watch TV, eat, whatever, everything seems to make me think of women." Then she got up and left.

The Mason was thinking about what just happened when a man sat down next to him, saw his ring and asked, "Are you a Mason?"

He replied, "I always thought I was, but I just found out I'm a lesbian."

The Lion

A WM and a PM were being chased by a hungry lion. The WM made some quick calculations, he said "It's no good trying to outrun it, its catching up".

The PM kept a little ahead and replied "I am not trying to outrun the lion, I am trying to outrun you!"

The Point

A Mason drinks a shot of whiskey every night before bed. After years of this, the wife wants him to quit; she gets two shot glasses, filling one with water and the other with whiskey.

After getting him to the table that had the glasses, she brings his bait box. She says "I want you to see this." She puts a worm in the water, and it swims around.

She puts a worm in the whiskey, and the worm dies immediately. She then says, feeling that she has made her point clear, "What do you have to say about this experiment?"

He responds by saying: "If I drink whiskey, I won't get worms!"

Shriner Fun

A completely inebriated Shriner was stumbling down the street with one foot on the curb and one foot in the gutter. A cop pulled up and said, "I've got to take you in, pal. You're obviously drunk."

Our wasted Shriner friend asked, "Officer, are ya absolutely sure I'm drunk?"

"Yeah, buddy, I'm sure," said the copper. "Let's go."

Breathing a sigh of relief, the Shriner said, "Thank goodness, I thought I was crippled."

Lawyer Logic

The local Masonic Lodge had a very publicized charity drive for its members. One day the lodge realized that they had never received a donation from the lodge's most successful lawyer. The person in charge of contributions called him to persuade him to contribute.

"Our research shows that out of a yearly income of at least $500,000, you give not a penny to charity. Wouldn't you like to give back to the community in some way?"

The lawyer mulled this over for a moment and replied, "First, did your research also show that my mother is dying after a long illness, and has medical bills that are several times her annual income?"

Embarrassed, the lodge rep mumbled, "Um ... no."

The lawyer interrupts, "or that my brother, a disabled Masonic veteran, is blind and confined to a wheelchair?"

The stricken lodge rep began to stammer out an apology, but was interrupted again.

".... or that my sister's husband died in a traffic accident," the lawyer's voice rising in indignation, "leaving her penniless with three children?!"

The humiliated lodge rep, completely beaten, said simply, "I had no idea..."

On a roll, the lawyer cut him off once again, "So if I don't give any money to them, why should I give any to you?"

Monks

There was this Mason who fell from an airplane and landed in a strange place. He was badly hurt and a couple of monks came and rescued him. And the Monks told the man to be careful because they were not going to save him again. The guy said okay then spent the night at the Monk's place. Later that night he heard an annoying loud banging and scratching sound that almost sounding like moaning. It was really loud. The next day he went back to the Monk's place and asked if they knew what the sound was. The Monk's Leader told the guy that he would have to be a monk to find out. The guy asked what it would take to be a monk. So the Monks told him that he would have to be there for eight years and pass a test.

So this guy stayed for eight years and finally passed the text. The guy asked again what that noise was he heard for so many years ago. The Monks agreed to tell him and told him to follow them. The guy was really happy because he lost a lot of sleep over that sound. He could sleep for years thinking about that noise that sounding almost like a heart beating. The Monks walked up to some big, huge doors and the noise kept getting louder and louder. So, loud that the Monks and the Guy couldn't hear each other. Do you want to know what was behind the doors?

I can't tell you! You're not a Monk!

The Name

A major research institution has recently announced the discovery of the heaviest chemical element yet known to science. The new element has been tentatively named "Provincialgrandlodgeium."

Provincialgrandlodgeium has one neutron, 12 assistant neutrons, 75 deputy neutrons, and 11 assistant deputy neutrons, giving it an atomic mass of 312.

These 312 particles are held together by forces called morons, which are surrounded by vast quantities of lepton-like particles called peons. Since Provincialgrandlodgeium has no electrons, it is inert.

However, it can be detected as it impedes every reaction with which it comes into contact. A minute amount of Provincialgrandlodgeium causes one reaction to take over four days to complete when it would normally take less than a second.

Provincialgrandlodgeium has a normal half-life of four years; it does not decay, but instead undergoes a reorganization in which a portion of the assistant neutrons and deputy neutrons exchange places. In fact, Provincialgrandlodgeium mass will actually increase over time, since each reorganization will cause more morons to become neutrons, forming isodopes. This characteristic of moron-promotion leads some scientists to speculate that Provincialgrandlodgeium is formed whenever morons reach a certain quantity in concentration. This hypothetical quantity is referred to as "Critical Morass." You will know it when you see it.

When catalyzed with money, Provincialgrandlodgeium becomes Grandlodgeium - an element which radiates just as much energy since it has half as many peons but twice as many morons.

She Knew Him

An elderly woman decided to prepare her will.

She told her husbands Lodge Almoner she had two final requests.

First, she wanted to be cremated, and second, she wanted her ashes scattered over the local Masonic Hall.

"The Masonic Hall!" the Almoner exclaimed. "Why the Masonic Hall?"

"Then I'll be sure my husband will visit me twice a week"

The Story

After receiving his first degree, a man returned home to his wife. Although he told her he couldn't talk about the degree, she kept pestering him to tell her something. He finally gave in and decided to tell her an outlandish story.

"Well," he said, "we put a naked woman on the altar and then dance in a circle around her."

"Do you look?" asked his wife.

"Of course I look," he said. "Otherwise I'd be an Oddfellow."

Law of Probability

The probability of a PM watching you during a Degree is proportional to the stupidity of your action.

Past Master Wisdom

Don't ignore the panhandler who asks you for a dime for a cup of coffee. Give it to him. Then follow him and find out where they still sell coffee for a dime.

Someone Important

A Masonic Lodge recently initiated several cannibals.

"You are all part of our team now", said the DC during the Festive Board.

"You are welcome to sit down at table to share our dinner, but please don't eat any of the members".

The cannibals promised they would not.

Four years later the PGM visited and remarked,

"You're all working very hard, and I'm quite satisfied with you. However, one of your Deacons has disappeared. Do any of you know what happened to him?"

The cannibals all shook their heads "no".

After the PGM had left, the leader of the cannibals said to the others,

"Which one of you idiots ate the Deacon?"

A hand rose hesitantly, to which the leader of the cannibals continued,

"You fool!!! For four years we've been eating Provincial Grand Officers and no one noticed anything, but NOOoooo, you had to go and eat someone important."

Points of View

American Masons: Seem to think that poverty & failure are morally suspect.

Canadian Masons: Seem to believe that wealth and success are morally suspect.

UK Masons: Seem to believe that wealth, poverty, success and failure are inherited things.

Aussie Masons: Seem to think that none of this matters after several beers.

A Poor Choice of Snack

Two tigers were stalking through the jungles of Asia. Suddenly, the one to the rear reached out with his tongue, and licked the posterior of the tiger in front of him. The startled front tiger turned and said, "Cut it out." The rear tiger apologized, and they continued onward.

About five minutes later, it happened again. The front tiger turned, growling, "I said stop it." The rear tiger again apologized, and they continued.

Another five minutes passed, and again the front tiger felt the unwanted tongue. The front tiger turned, giving the rear tiger a ferocious glare, angrily hissing, "What is it with you?"

The rear tiger replied, "I'm sorry -- I really didn't mean to offend you. But I just ate a Shriner and I'm trying to get the taste out of my mouth!"

Brotherly Love

A Doctor and Plumber are in the same Lodge. On Sunday Morning the Doctor wakes up to find his toilet blocked. So he rings the Plumber.

"But I don't work Sundays! Can't it wait until tomorrow."

The Doctor said. "I don't like working Sundays either but if you were in trouble, and felt unwell, Brother I would come round to see you"

"OK" says the Plumber and goes round to the Doctor. Goes upstairs and looks at the toilet, take two aspirins from his pocket and throws them down the bowl. "There" he says "If it's no better tomorrow give me a ring and I will call round."

Understandable

While visiting a newly initiated brother at home one day, the new brother's wife took me to one side and said her husband had started behaving very strange since joining.
I asked in what way?
She said that he locks himself in the toilet for hours on end mumbling to himself with his little blue book.
Later that evening I turned the talk to lodge, and asked him how he was getting on.
Oh fine was his reply.
I asked him about his behavior and if there was anything wrong.
No, was his reply.
So why read the book there?
Well he said "Its the only TYLED room in the house"....

Light/Lite

A small Lodge had had a string of bad luck. It was preparing to initiate a candidate on a steamy evening in June and it's air conditioner had stopped working. After sweating their way through part of the work, the Master had asked the candidate what he most desired.

The candidate replied "a beer".

At this juncture the WM., being startled, whispered "light" to the candidate.

"OK," the candidate replied, "a lite beer."

Gotca!

This dog, is dog, a dog, good dog, way dog, to dog, keep dog, a dog, Mason dog, busy dog, for dog, 20 dog, seconds dog! ...

Now read without the word "dog".

This and That

How do stop a Grand Lodge Officer drinking?
Slam the lid down on his head!

How many Masons does it take to change a light bulb?
None! They would all rather sit around and talk about how good the old one was!

New Brother : "why is a mother lodge so called?"
Past Master : "Well, it always expects."

The Library

A pair of chickens wearing Masonic aprons walk up to a Masonic Temple and make their way into the library. They go up to the librarian and say, 'Buk Buk BUK.' The librarian decides that the chickens desire three books, and gives it to them...and the chickens leave shortly thereafter.

Around midday, the two chickens return to the libraryquite vexed and say,' Buk Buk BuKKOOK!' The librarian decides that the chickens desire another three books and gives it to them. The chickens leave as before.

The two chickens return to the library in the early after-noon, approach the librarian, looking very annoyed and say, 'Buk Buk Buk Buk Bukkooook!' The librarian is now a little suspicious of these chickens. She gives them what they request, and decides to follow them.

He followed them out of the Themple, down the street, and to a park. At this point, he hid behind a tree, not wanting to be seen. He saw the two chickens throwing the books at a frog wearing an apron in a pond, to which the frog was saying, "Rrredit Rrredit Rrredit..."

Story of My brother

I have a lodge brother who is a pilot on a 747.
I said "Hi Jack."
He shot me.

The Bar

Three Masons are walking down the street and then two of them walk into a bar. The third one ducks.

The Dying Past Master

A Past Master on his deathbed called his friend and said, "Brother Bill, I want you to promise me that when I die you will have my remains cremated."

"And what," his friend asked, "do you want me to do with your ashes?"

The PM said, "Just put them in an envelope and mail them to the Internal Revenue Service. Write on the envelope, "Now, you have everything."

Worthy Patrons

How's a Worthy Patron like a dead body at a funeral?

You can't hold the meeting without him, but nobody expects him to do or say much.

Worthy Patrons Again

The Eastern Star held a seminar about getting new members. During a break a brother happened to overhear one Worthy Matron say to another, "Ours is up ten." The second Worthy Matron responded, "We've got you beat. Our gain is twenty-five."

The brother said, "Pardon me, sisters. I don't mean to interrupt, but I couldn't help hearing. That's wonderful news! Between your chapters we've got thirty-five new members!"

"New members?" said the first, "We were talking about how many pounds our Worthy Patrons have gained this year."

And Now the Shriners

There was an incident recently involving a policeman and a car full of Shriners he pulled over for speeding. As he approached the car, he noticed they were all wearing fezzes.

He said to them, "Oh, you are all shriners aren't you? Well, I will let you off the hook this time because you guys do a lot of good. Had you been a bunch of Masons, I would have run you all in.

The Shriners Again

Three Shriners were standing in line to get into heaven one day. Apparently it had been a pretty busy day, though, so St. Peter had to tell the first one, "Heaven's getting pretty close to full today, and I've been asked to admit only people who have had particularly horrible deaths. So what's your story?"

The first man replies: "Well, for a while I've suspected my wife has been cheating on me, so today I came home early to try to catch her red-handed. As I came into my 25th floor apartment, I could tell something was wrong, but all my searching around didn't reveal where this other guy could have been hiding. Finally, I went out to the balcony, and sure enough, there was this man hanging off the railing, 25 floors above ground! By now I was really mad, so I started beating on him and kicking him, but wouldn't you know it, he wouldn't fall off. So finally I went back into my apartment and got a hammer and starting hammering on his fingers. Of course, he couldn't stand that for long, so he let go and fell-but even after 25 stories, he fell into the bushes, stunned but okay. I couldn't stand it anymore, so I ran into the kitchen, grabbed the fridge, and threw it over the edge where it landed on him, killing him instantly. But all the stress and anger got to me, and I had a heart attack and died there on the balchoy."

"That sounds like a pretty bad day to me," said Peter, and let the man in.

The second man comes up and Peter explains to him about heaven being full, and again asks for his story.

"It's been a very strange day. You see, I live on the 26th floor of my apartment building, and every morning I do my exercises out on my balcony. Well, this morning I must have slipped or something, because I fell over the edge. But I got lucky, and caught the railing of the balcony on the floor below me. I knew I couldn't hang on for very long, when suddenly this man burst out onto the balcony. I thought for sure I was saved, when he started beating on me and kicking me. I held on the best I could until he ran into the apartment and grabbed a hammer and started pounding on my hands. Finally I just let go, but again I got lucky and fell into the bushes below, stunned but all right. Just when I was thinking I was going to be okay, this refrigerator comes falling out of the sky and crushes me instantly, and now I'm here."
Once again, Peter had to concede that that sounded like a pretty horrible death.

The third man came to the front of the line, and St. Peter asked for his story.

"Picture this," says the third man, "I'm hiding naked inside a refrigerator...

Joining Woes

It was a sad, sad day when the Masonic Lodge burned to the ground. The brothers were having a new lodge built, but in the interim, they had no place to go for regular meetings. One of the members owned a hotel and figured they could use the conference room in his hotel for their meetings. They agreed and met there regularly. Four months pass and a traveling salesman is passing through town and decides to stay at the hotel. As luck would have it, he was checking in on one of the lodge meeting nights. He spied the men in white aprons filing into the conference room and asked the deskclerk,

"I say, are those freemasons?" The clerk replied that they were and explained about the lodge burning down and the subsequent use of the hotel for meetings.

"Well," said the salesman, "I've been thinking about joining. Do you think it's hard to do so?" The clerk shrugged,

"I'd say it's pretty tough. You see that guy standing by the door with a sword? Well, he's been knocking on that door for four months now and they still won't let him in."

EA Hunters

Two EAs go hunting. Soon they get separated and, as often happens, one mistakes the other for a deer and shoots him. After much effort he drags his buddy from the woods, throws him in the 4x4 and takes him to the nearest hospital.

"Will he be all right?" the worried EA asks the doctor.

"It's hard to say," says the doctor. "But it would have been better if you hadn't gutted and skinned him."

Fishing for a Week

A WM of a lodge phones home from the office and tells his wife, "Something has just come up and the lodge officers all have the chance to go fishing for a week. It's the opportunity of a lifetime. We leave right away, so can you pack my clothes, my fishing equipment, and especially my blue silk pajamas? I'll be home in an hour to pick them up."

He hurries home, grabs everything and rushes off.

A week later he returns. His wife asks, "Did you have a good trip?"

"Oh yes, great! But you forgot to pack my blue silk pajamas."

"Oh no I didn't. I put them in your tackle box."

Arm Troubles

A Mason went to visit his doctor. "Doc, my arm hurts bad. Can you check it out please?" the man pleads.

The doctor rolls up the man's sleeve and suddenly hears the arm talk.

"Hello, Doctor." says the arm. "Could you lend me twenty bucks please? I'm desperate!"

"Aha!' says the doctor.

'I see the problem. Your arm is broke!"

The Husband Store

A store that sells husbands has just opened where a woman may go to choose a husband from among many men. The store is composed of 6 floors, and the men increase in positive attributes as the shopper ascends the flights.

There is, however, a catch. As you open the door to any floor you may choose a man from that floor, but if you go up a floor, you cannot go back down except to exit the building.

So a woman goes to the shopping center to find a husband.

On the first floor the sign on the door reads:

Floor 1 - These men are Freemasons and have jobs.

The woman reads the sign and says to herself, "Well, that's better than my last boyfriend, but I wonder what's further up?" So up she goes.

The second floor sign reads:

Floor 2 - These men are Freemasons, have jobs and love kids.

The woman remarks to herself, "That's great, but I wonder what's further up?" And up she goes again.

The third floor sign reads:

Floor 3 - These men are Freemasons, have jobs, love kids and are extremely good looking.

"Hmmm, better" she says. "But I wonder what's upstairs?"

The fourth floor sign reads:

Floor 4 - These men are Freemasons, have jobs, love kids, are extremely good looking and help with the housework.

"Wow!" exclaims the woman, "very tempting. BUT, there must be more further up!" And again she heads up another flight.

The fifth floor sign reads:

Floor 5 - These men are Freemasons, have jobs, love kids, are extremely good looking, help with the housework and have a strong romantic streak.

"Oh, mercy me! But just think... what must be awaiting me further on?" So up to the sixth floor she goes.

The sixth floor sign reads:

Floor 6 - You are visitor 6,875,953,012 to this floor. There are no men on this floor. This floor exists solely as proof that women are impossible to please.

Masons and the Blonde

A blonde was sick and tired of people making fun of her for being a blonde, so she decided to hang herself.

A couple minutes later two Masons walk by and see her hanging by her wrists.

"What are you doing." they ask her.

So she replies "Hanging myself."

The men are confused and asked "If you are hanging youself, you put the rope around your neck."

The blonde says "Duh....I tried that, I couldn't breath."

The Teeth

This Freemason was preparing to go to a meeting where he was giving a lecture. As he was getting ready he forgot to put in his false teeth, and left the house without them.

It was only when he was on the train, going over his notes, he realised his error. The man sitting opposite noticed his discomforture and asked him what was the problem. After explaining, the man opposite said he was going to the same meeting, and may be able to help. Whereon he felt in his left jacket pocket, and pulled out a set of false teeth. The man tried them, but they were too loose, so the other man felt in his right pocket and brought out a second pair, which proved too large.

Having tried both and not proving OK, the man opposite went through his case and brought out a third pair, which fitted perfectly. The man giving the speech was delighted and exclaimed, "This is a miracle, I leave my teeth at home, and find on this train the only man that can help me is in my compartment, but is also a dentist". At this the man opposite said, "I am not a dentist, I am a Funeral Director"!!

How about this?

How many Masons does it take to change a light bulb?
None! They would all rather sit around and talk about how good the old one was!

New Brother : "why is a mother lodge so called?"
Past Master : "Well, it always expects."

Hot Lodge

One hot, summer night two muffins are in Lodge and the air is broken. One says to the other "God, it's hot in here." The other one replies "Oh no... It's a talking muffin"

The Long Meeting

A Mason is on a Business Trip. One day he comes to a small village, somewhere in the north of England. Our Brother is curious to know whether there is a Masonic Lodge or not, so he takes a walk through the village and after some time he finds a path called "Mason's Road."

Thinking that the path might lead to the Masonic Temple, he follows it. At the end of the pathway he sees a building, which looks somewhat rotten and seems to have been out of use for quite a while. Our Brother tries to open the door and, surprisingly, it is not locked. He goes inside and finds dust and spider webs everywhere. In front a door there sits a skeleton, wearing an apron , a collar and holding a sword in its hand.

"O my God", thinks our Brother and enters the Lodge room. In puzzlement, he sees skeletons with collars and aprons everywhere. The W.M., the Wardens, the Organist, Deacons - all skeletons. He looks around and goes to the seats of the Secretary and Treasurer.

Under the hand of the Treasurer he finds a small piece of paper, a little note, which he seems to have passed to the Secretary. So our Brother picks up the note, blows away the dust and reads: "If nobody prompts the W.M., we will sit here forever!"

The "Funny" Ring

Two friends were riding the train to work. Frank said to John, "Did you ever notice the conductor never takes a ticket from that guy wearing that funny ring. I've seen those rings in the pawn shop. I think I'll get me one and see what happens".

The next day Frank was flashing his new ring when the conductor came up and asked him, "Will you be off or from?"

Frank thought for a moment then replied "I'll be off".

The conductor told him he was right. He put him off at the next station.

It's MINE!

One day an English mason, a Scottish mason, and an Irish mason were in the bar after the meeting.

They each proceeded to buy a pint of Guinness.

Just as they were about to enjoy their creamy beverage, a fly landed in each of their pints and became stuck in the thick head.

The Englishman pushed his beer from him in disgust.

The Irishman fished the offending fly out of his beer and continued drinking it as if nothing had happened.

The Scotsman picked the fly out of his drink, held it out over the beer and yelled

"SPIT IT OUT!! SPIT IT OUT!!!!"

A Woman and a Shriner

A woman and a Shriner get into a car accident. Both of their cars are totally demolished, but amazingly neither of them is hurt.

After they crawl out of the wreckage, the woman says, "Wow, look at our cars - there's nothing left! Thank God we are all right. This must be a sign from Him that we should be friends and not try to pin the blame on each other."

The Shriner replies, "Oh yes, I agree with you completely."

The woman points to a bottle on the ground and says, "And here's another miracle. Somehow this bottle of Scotch from my back seat didn't break. Surely God wants us to drink this Scotch and celebrate our good fortune."

Then she hands the bottle to the Shriner. The Shriner nods his head in agreement, opens it, and chugs about a third of the bottle to calm his nerves. He then hands it back to the woman. The woman takes the bottle, immediately puts the cap back on, and hands it back to him.

The Shriner asks, "Aren't you having any?"

The woman replies, "No. I think I'll just wait for the police..."

Masonic Wishes

A Mason is walking down the beach and comes across an old bottle. He picks it up, pulls out the cork and out pops a genie. The genie says "Thank you for freeing me from the bottle. In return I will grant you three wishes."

The Mason says "Great. I always dreamed of this and I know exactly what I want. First, I want 1 Billion dollars in a Swiss bank account."

Phoof! There is a flash of light and a piece of paper with account numbers appears in his hand.

He continues, "Next, I want a brand new red Ferrari right here."

Phoof! There is a flash of light and abright red brand-new Ferrari appears right next to him.

He continues, "Finally, I want to be irresistible to women."

Phoof! There is a flash of light and he turns into a box of chocolates

When in Ireland

An American Mason was in Ireland. On his way to Belfast, he stopped at a bar and asked one of the locals, "What's the quickest way to Belfast?"

The Irishmen asked, "Are you walking or driving?"

The Mason replied, "I'm driving!"

The Irishman said, "Aye, that'd be the quickest way!"

3 plus 3

3 French Masons and 3 English Masons are travelling by train to a conference. At the station, the 3 English Masons each buy tickets and watch as the 3 French Masons buy only a single ticket. "How are 3 people going to travel on only one ticket?" asks one English Mason. "Watch and you'll see." answers one French Mason. They all board the train. The English Masons take their respective seats but all three French Masons cram into a restroom and close the door behind them. Shortly after the train has departed, the conductor comes around collecting tickets. He knocks on the restroom door and says, "Ticket, please." The door opens just a crack and a single arm emerges with a ticket in hand. The conductor takes it and moves on. The English Masons saw this and agreed it was quite a clever idea. So after the conference, the English Masons decide to copy the French Masons on the return trip and save some money (being clever with money, and all that). When they get to the station, they buy a single ticket for the return trip. To their astonishment, the French Masons don't buy a ticket at all. "How are you going to travel without a ticket?" says one perplexed English Mason. "Watch and you'll see." answers a French Mason. When they board the train the 3 English Masons cram into a restroom and the 3 French Masons cram into another one nearby. The train departs. Shortly afterward, one of the French Masons leaves his restroom and walks over to the restroom where the English Masons are hiding. He knocks on the door and says, "Ticket, please."

The Templars

Q: How do you stop 26 Masonic Knights Templar on horseback?

A: Turn off the carousel.

The Tunnel

A Mason, a Knight of Columbus, a girl and an old woman are traveling on a train that has just entered a dark tunnel.

Suddenly they hear a loud slap, and when the train emerges, the Knight of Columbus has a red hand print on his cheek.

"He must have groped the girl, and she slapped him." the old woman thinks.

"He tried to grope me but fondled the old lady instead, and she slapped him." the girl decides.

"The Mason must have groped the blonde, and she slapped me by accident." the Knight of Columbus determines.

"I can't wait for another tunnel," the Mason thinks, "so I can smack that Knight of Columbus again!"

Picture This!

A PM goes skydiving. After a fantastic free fall he pulls the rip cord to open his parachute but nothing happens. He tries everything but can't get it open.

Just then another man flies by him, going UP. The skydiver yells, "Hey, you know anything about parachutes?

The man replies, "No, you know anything about gas stoves?

Swimming Dog

A little boy's dog swims out to see and gets into difficulties in the big waves.

The little boy screams: "Help! Help! My little dog is drowning!"

A passing Jewish Mason hears his pathetic cries, sees the poor dog and leaps into the sea fully clothed. He swims out, grabs the dog, swims back to shore and gives to dog mouth-to-mouth. The dog is saved and runs off happily.

"O thank you, thank you," says the little boy. "You must be a vet."

"Am I a vet? I'm more than a vet, I'm a-soaking," exclaims the Jewish Brother.

5645493R00054

Printed in Great Britain
by Amazon.co.uk, Ltd.,
Marston Gate.